From
COSMOS
to
CRADLE

Meditations on the Incarnation

From
COSMOS
to
CRADLE

Meditations on the Incarnation

BRUCE G. EPPERLY

ANAMCHARA
BOOKS

Anamchara Books
Vestal, New York 13850
www.AnamcharaBooks.com

Scripture quotations are from the New Revised Standard Version
Bible, copyright © 1989 National Council of the Churches of
Christ in the United States of America. Used by permission. All
rights reserved worldwide. The author has, however, altered certain
scriptural passages to make their language inclusive (as he believes
Jesus would have done as a matter of affirmation and hospitality).

Print ISBN: 978-1-62524-848-0
eBook ISBN: 978-1-62524-849-7

Cover design by Ellyn Sanna.

CONTENTS

ACKNOWLEDGMENTS

I am grateful for the support of Westmoreland Congregational United Church of Christ pastors Tim Tutt and Kaeley McEvoy as well as class members from Bethesda, Maryland; Lancaster, Pennsylvania; Washington, DC; and Cape Cod, Massachusetts. Carole Green-Weishaupt inspired me to consider writing this book, when as one class concluded, she chimed, "I bet a book will come of these lectures." And so, it did! I am grateful to the work of Marcus Borg and John Dominic Crossan in *First Christmas* for providing political, sociological, and cultural context to complement my theo-spiritual adventures. I am also thankful for my partner Kate Epperly who has made our new suburban townhouse a home and fitted out a comfortable study and library for my classes and ruminations, and to my father and mother who first taught me these stories, and to my son and grandchildren with whom I shared them. A philosopher and theologian without love is spiritually dead, and I am spiritually alive through the love of Kate, my grandchildren, and my son and his wife. *Ubuntu*: I am because of you; we are because of one another.

AN INVITATION
TO ADVENTURE

The stories of Christmas have always captivated me. As a child, I was mesmerized by images of the star, shepherds, magi, and the animals who attended Jesus' birth. Christmas pageants were the norm in my childhood, and I have participated in the pageantry of Christmas, bathrobes and all, virtually every year since childhood. At home, I begin to play Christmas carols on Thanksgiving weekend and continue through the Feast of Epiphany. A guilty pleasure, often the source of teasing from friends, is my delight in Hallmark Christmas movies, and their yearly Christmas miracles of romance and healed relationships. I delight in the yearly rituals of watching *It's a Wonderful Life* and *A Christmas Carol*. The producers and writers of these movies know we all need a happy ending—a demonstration that love conquers all in our ambiguous and uncertain world. We need good to triumph over evil, whether in a saccharine movie or in the affairs of persons and nations. We need to believe we can change course like Ebenezer Scrooge and grow our hearts three sizes like the Grinch who stole Christmas.

The stories of Jesus' birth are more mysterious than modern Christmas narratives. They take us beyond the world of rational analysis and scientific method. Even though the Gospel accounts of Jesus' birth share features with the birth stories of other great religious and national leaders—the miraculous birth, the mother and child, threat from political powers, and dramatic Divine interventions—the Christmas stories uniquely capture the hope and dream of Emmanuel, God with us, incarnate in the vulnerability of an infant, the challenges of domestic life, the despair and alienation of those society judges as nuisances and nobodies, as well as in the machinations of the great and near great, the potentates and the prevaricators. In the great challenges of life, the Incarnation evokes the joy of shepherds and magi, the leaping fetus John and his parents Elizabeth and Zechariah, the weary parents for whom the birth makes the arduous journey worthwhile, and for us today, the hope and joy of new life amid the realities of war, poverty, division, and oppression. The echoes of Christmas past resound in this present moment with hope of new life: "Joy to the world, the Lord *is* come!"

"God became flesh and lives with us" is the mantra of Christmas. The Incarnate Word and Wisdom of God in a little baby. Godhead in diapers. The triumph of love over hate, and light over darkness. These are primordial human hopes and, as the carol proclaims, in Bethlehem, "the hopes and fears of all the years are met in thee tonight"—tonight, in Bethlehem, in today's war-torn nations and refugee camps, in occupied Palestine, and in the violent and divided United States.

As a rather trite Christmas song asserts, "We need a little Christmas, right this very moment." We need the spirit of Christmas not only in December but also in July. Too many of us struggle to understand the amazing details of the Christmas story. Our rational mind counteracts our intuitive spirit. In our minds and churches, the disenchanted, horizontal, and unimaginative modern worldview challenges the lively, multidimensional, and unpredictable enchanted perspective of the Christmas stories.

In our struggle to fathom the mysteries of incarnation, we are searching for something more than the unimaginative literalism of fundamentalists and the curmudgeonly analyses of biblical scholars. We are aware of the poetic license that places the magi and shepherds beside one another in the Christmas tableau. We also wrestle with the notion of the Virgin Birth and the gymnastic attempts to exempt Mary of Nazareth from the taint of original sin. Still, we don't want to throw the baby out with the bath water, literally and figuratively. Incarnation is always more than we can imagine and expresses the deepest truths of life, despite apparent factual inaccuracies.

We need a sense of miracle and radical amazement. We need the doors of perception cleansed and thrown open to see the Infinity within our daily chores. We need dusty shepherds, regal magi, and reverent farm animals to liberate the wellsprings of empathy from our Scrooge-like attempts to manage reality. We may doubt the stories of supernatural interventions, upsetting the dependable cause-and-effect relationships necessary for navigating everyday life—and yet we deeply need a vision of the miraculous. We yearn for images of something beyond and more enduring than the violence perpetrated by school shooters, prevaricating politicians, death-filled dictators, and planet polluters. Only a miracle can save us from hopelessness: the miracle of unexpected possibilities and the energy and courage to pursue them. The miracle of God's presence in a vulnerable baby.

Stories are full of wisdom we take away with us. A hobbit discovers that not all who wander are lost. Henry Potter experiences the wonders hidden behind Gate 9 ¾. Four children find their vocation as heroes when they pass through a wardrobe to Narnia. We discover, as we ponder our own quest for infinity in finite life, that, in the hopeful affirmations of Mahatma Gandhi and June Jordan, we can become the change we want to see in the world and that we—and not some political savior or all-knowing guru or celebrity spiritual guide—are the ones we've been waiting for. Stories like these give us hope, courage, and inspiration.

The Christmas stories send us on a vision quest, a holy adventure, in which we may see strange beasts, encounter angels, and battle demons—and in the process discover the holiness of our own lives. The hopes and fears of all the years dwell within us, and more than that, the Christ Child, the humble Baby, is also waiting to be born in us, inviting us to be midwives of a new Earth, embodying the contours of a new Heaven, both within and beyond our individual adventures. The Incarnation and the Christmas story point to a Divine reality whose birthday is more expansive than one day in December, and wider even than Christianity itself.

The Christmas reflections of this book emerged in a Zoom class, sponsored by Westmoreland Congregational United Church of Christ in Bethesda, Maryland, and attended online by persons across the United States. These meditations are intended to be spiritual as well as intellectual, devotional, and historical. Although I am a trained theologian, deeply rooted in scholarship, I believe with Pascal that "the heart has reasons that reason knows nothing of." Mysticism must be grounded in the real world of historical evidence, while illuminating everyday life. The mystics know the "thin places" in our everyday world where Divinity and humanity meet, and the finite realizes the Infinite that undergirds our personal lives and planetary history.

These reflections emerged from the marriage of heart, mind, and intuition. They are an expedition in what I call "theo-spirituality," the affirmation that theology has its origins in mystical experiences and that theological reflection shapes the contours of our spiritual practices and illuminates our encounters with the Holy. I have studied these stories as an academic pastor for over four decades, seeking to join the pulpit and study in preaching, teaching, adult and children's faith formation, and spiritual direction. I have pored over academic treatises, but in writing this book, my approach has been to reflect on a story each night before going to bed, asking for Divine guidance and an unfettered imagination. I assumed that the world of dreams, so dear to the Gospel writers, was also the world of insight and inspiration. Upon awakening each morning, following my morning prayer and meditation time, I let the words flow, joining inspiration, intuition, and intellect, inviting the miraculous Incarnation to come forth in the intersection of heart and mind. After my morning writing, I set off on an hour's walk in my Potomac, Maryland, neighborhood, returning to the text with fresh ideas inspired by the tree-lined paths I traversed.

In the spirit of the theo-spirituality that motivates these reflections, each meditation concludes with a contemplative practice that joins theology and spirituality in your quest to incarnate God's word and wisdom in your daily life. These practices are incarnational, not otherworldly, and are intended to illuminate your world, inspire the fire of passion, and challenge you to bring light and love to your relationships and citizenship.

And so, the journey begins. Star, sheep and cattle, strangers from a strange land, shepherds, and an ordinary yet amazing family: these will be our companions as we prayerfully seek a star on the horizon, training our ears to hear the carols of angels:

> O Holy Child of Bethlehem
> Descend to us, we pray
> Cast out our sin and enter in
> Be born in us today.

We hear the Christmas angels
The great glad tidings tell
O come to us, abide with us
Our Lord Emmanuel.

Loving God, be born in us.
Help us to experience the old stories in new ways.
Let the radical amazement of Jesus' birth
illuminate our lives and awaken us
to the glory of each moment of life.
In the name of the Christ Child. Amen.

MEDITATION ONE

FROM COSMOS TO CRADLE

In the beginning was the Word, and the Word was with God, and the Word was God. The Word was in the beginning with God. All things came into being through the Word, and without Divine Wisdom not one thing came into being. What has come into being in God was life, and the life was the light of all people. The light shines in the darkness, and the darkness did not overtake it. . . . The true light, which enlightens everyone, was coming into the world. (John 1:1–5, 9)

Former Speaker of the United States House of Representatives Tip O'Neill once asserted that all politics is local. While it's true that people make decisions based on their concrete day-to-day experiences, today we know that the local is also the global, and the global is personal.

What happens in China or Ukraine can turn U.S. economics and way of life upside down. A butterfly flapping its wings in Pacific Grove can shape the weather patterns in suburban Washington, DC, where I live. Philosopher Alfred North Whitehead declared that the whole universe conspires to create each moment of experience, and the intricate interdependence of life applies to souls, cells, and planets.

The author of John's Gospel, written about a hundred years after Jesus' birth, sixty years after the end of Jesus' active ministry, makes a bold claim for the coming of Christ, the healer and messiah. While the Gospel of John, like the Gospel of Mark, reports nothing about Jesus' birth, the Gospel roots Jesus the Christ in the cosmic context of God's omnipresent and omni-active creative wisdom. Divine creativity gives birth to the universe, the myriad galaxies (a trillion and counting), our solar system, planet Earth, and every moment of experience.

Life begins with the creative wisdom of God. The Gospel of John is unconcerned with the age of the Earth or the universe. Although John may have affirmed the ancient vision of a three-story universe—heaven, earth, and the underworld—he was not wedded to any specific cosmic or planetary timetable. No doubt John was well-versed in the Genesis 1 creation story and its affirmation of the goodness of the world, and the "six-day" evolutionary process that joins the grand vision of creation out of chaos with the emergence of life on Earth, culminating in the creation of humankind in the Divine image. Surely John also delighted in the Proverbs 8 account of the Father's creative partnership with Chokmah or Sophia, the feminine wisdom of God whose artistry brings forth the Earth, stars, sun, and creaturely life.

> The LORD created me at the beginning of God's work, the first of his acts of long ago. Ages ago I was set up, at the first, before the beginning of the earth. When God established the heavens, I was there; when God drew a circle on the face of the deep, when God made firm the skies above, when God established the fountains of the deep, when God assigned to the sea its limit, so that the waters might not transgress his command, when God marked out the foundations of the earth, then I was beside God, like a master worker, and I was daily God's delight, playing before God always, playing in God's inhabited world and delighting in the human race. (Proverbs 8:22–31)

The universe envisioned by John is inherently moral and spiritual, the product of Divine wisdom. As Psalm 104 proclaims, "in wisdom all is made." Wisdom is also playful and delightful, as well as tragic and beautiful. The quest for beauty and Shalom[1] is embedded in the process that brings forth suns and stars, polar bears and pangolins, humankind and the holy adventures of spirituality and science. The moral and spiritual arcs that move through human history, luring humanity toward God's vision of Shalom, also guide the vastness of the cosmic adventure. Humankind is part of a larger cosmic adventure, guided by the Light of the World, embodied in Christ.

Chaos and conflict exist and are fundamental to the emergence of life and human decision-making. Persons may tragically prefer darkness over light, and nations succumb to power plays and prevarication (see John 1:10–11). Still, the creative light of the world, the light of Divine wisdom, persists in shaping human and cosmic adventures in ways that lean toward beauty and justice. "The light shines in the darkness, and the darkness did not overtake it" (John 1:5).

John's prologue to his Gospel doesn't mention the historical Jesus or even invoke the name of Jesus. The mission of Jesus is implicit, however, in everything the Fourth Gospel proclaims. Jesus is not an anomaly in universal history, but the ultimate manifestation of the moral and spiritual arcs that give rise to planets, persons, and politics. John's Jesus is the Alpha and Omega, the ultimate pattern and goal of human existence and the historical process. Wherever there is truth and healing, the wisdom present in Jesus is at work. God became human, as early Christian theologians asserted, so that humankind might become Divine.

God's wisdom prepares a way for human wholeness. God's wisdom is the life that gives light to all people, even those who succumb to the lures of chaos and conflict. The impact of Jesus' life and message is not restricted to Christianity but the Christ, the incarnation of Sophia and Logos, gives birth and inspires every authentic spiritual path and every faith tradition. "The true light, which enlightens everyone, was coming into the world" (John 1:9). In the spirit of Isaiah's mystical experience in the Temple, John affirms that despite human sinfulness and ignorance, "the whole earth is full of God's glory" (Isaiah 6:3). There is a Godward movement in all things that cannot be stifled by human recalcitrance. "The light shines in the darkness, and the darkness did not overtake it" (John 1:5).

John's prologue joins metaphysics and mysticism. Spiritual experiences enable us to perceive God's light, and God's light reveals the meaning and goal of the cosmic process. We are not, as Walker Pearcy avers, "lost in the cosmos." The cosmos is our home, and though we are latecomers, living on a pale, blue dot at the edges of the Milky Way, we are only a little lower than the Divine and have been given the task of guiding creation (Psalm 8). The world is on fire with the passion of Divine love, and the energy of love enables us to heal the sick, confront injustice with loving power, and fathom the universe. From cosmos to cradle, God's energy of love and guiding wisdom inspires and ignites all creation, moving us from self-interested apathy to world-loyal empathy.

As a child, I delighted in singing "This Little Light of Mine." The simple words embody Jesus' affirmation: "You are the light of the world. Let your light shine." The song took flesh as the Civil Rights movement adapted it as an antidote to fear and injustice. May we too let our lights shine.

CONTEMPLATION

After a time of quiet reflection on Matthew 5:13–16, breathe deeply, letting God's breath fill you from head to toe. Visualize God's breath as a light inspiring, enlivening, and igniting you, energizing you for God's call in your life. As you exhale, breathe God's light into the world. See this light healing the soul of the nation and the planet. Experience this light enveloping with healing love persons in need, whether Ukrainian refugees or refugees along the U.S. border or families traumatized by gun violence. Feel the light also encircling someone from whom you are alienated in your personal or political life. This could be a foreign dictator, a seditious American politician, or a corporate leader who puts profits before planetary well-being. Let this energy encircle you protectively, as you ask God for guidance in ways to bring your light to the world in healing and reconciling ways. Ask God to let the light of Christ fill and inspire you throughout the day as you give thanks for God's blessings in your life.

Light of the world,

shine in me. Shine through me.

Guide my thoughts and my steps

in ways of peace and healing.

Encircle me with protection

and give me courage to be your companion

in healing the Earth.

In the name of the Light Giver. Amen.

THE WORD WAS MADE FLESH

To all who received him, who believed in his name, he gave power to become children of God, who were born, not of blood or of the will of the flesh or of the will of man, but of God. And the Word became flesh and lived among us, and we have seen his glory, the glory as of a father's only son, full of grace and truth. No one has ever seen God. It is the only Son, himself God, who is close to the Father's heart, who has made him known. (John 1:12–14, 18)

S aint Francis and his followers believed that the heart of spirituality involved lovingly embracing "God and all things." God speaks to us in gentle winds, warms us with passionate fire, serenades us with the hymns of sparrows, and heals us with compassionate touch. For Francis, the skin of lepers became sacramental, and just one touch healed their spirits. A wolf that was attacking the village of Gubbio became a spiritual companion when Francis looked the wolf in the eye and made the sign of the Cross. All creation praises God, because God moves through all things—body, mind, spirit, relationships. Heaven and earth jointly declare God's glory. We may turn from God, preferring the self-centered desires of our own hearts, but the Light always turns toward us.

German mystic Meister Eckhardt affirmed all things as "words of God," revealing the wisdom and creativity of their Creator. Rhineland spiritual guide Hildegard of Bingen delighted in the green liveliness of the good Earth, and priest-paleontologist Teilhard de Chardin imagined the inner spirit giving passionate birth to the outer expression of cosmic evolution.

The Word is made flesh. God has skin, cells, a reproductive system, and a circulatory system. God's touch heals, and God's voice calms and inspires. Our souls and cells equally reveal God's omnipresent and omni-active artistry. The Poet of the Universe is embodied. The Spirit of the Universe is enfleshed. Incarnation reveals the marriage of Creator and creature in all its messiness. Embodiment in all its wonder declares the glory of God.

Jesus, a flesh-and-blood baby, is wrapped in swaddling clothes and lies in a manger. The Incarnation of God, fully alive in human flesh, full of Divine grace and beauty, thirsts, tires, sleeps, urinates and defecates, grows, suffers, and dies. A God with skin feels the lash of the whip and the agony of nails pounded into flesh.

All Earth is filled with God's glory, and God's glory embraces and seeks to heal the suffering of the world. God is our fellow sufferer who understands, as well as the loving companion who celebrates.

We are called to love God in the world of the flesh, for God loves the world. Reflecting on God's diverse, messy, embodied, sexy, and wonderful creativity, Alice Walker's Shug, in *The Color Purple*, claims that true worship involves noticing God's creation with wonder and gratitude: "I think it pisses God off if you walk by the color purple in a field somewhere and don't notice it. People think pleasing God is all God cares about. But any fool living in the world can see it always trying to please us back."

The Universe is the Body of Christ. The Divine revealed in Christ is the Spirit of the Universe. God's body is not dense and dead matter, but lively, wise, and intelligent energy. Just as holistic medicine has discovered that the human mind and the molecules of emotion are present everywhere in the body, so the Divine Mind energizes every cell in the Body of the Universe. The Divine shapes the currents of universal experience, and the universe shapes the currents of God's experience.

You are the embodiment of Divine Wisdom, as Jesus was. Psalm 139 proclaims about each of us:

> For it was you who formed my inward parts; you knit me together in my mother's womb. I praise you, for I am fearfully and wonderfully made. Wonderful are your works; that I know very well. (Psalm 139:13–14)

All of us are God's children, God's beloved, receiving God's enlightenment. We are awesome and miraculous in the intricacies of our bodies, minds, and spirits. Those who turn to the Light, letting it shape their lives, are given the power to become children of God—in other words, fully experience the energy of love in their lives. Filled with God's spirit, they can do great things and transform the world. The Light shines in them, inspiring them to be God's lights in the world (Matthew 5:13–16).

From the cosmic point of view, our knowledge of the moral and spiritual arcs of the universe, the ultimate meaning of the universe, comes in beholding Jesus the Christ. "No one has ever seen God. It is the only Son, himself God, who is close to the Father's heart, who has made him known" (John

1:18). We live in a Christ-formed, Christ-guided universe. The deepest reality of human existence and the universe is Christ-like. God in Christ is the energy in the moral and spiritual evolution of the universe, who calls us to claim our vocations as companions in promoting the evolutionary process.

One of the most well-known scriptures is John 3:16: "For God so loved that world that God gave God's only begotten child so that everyone who believes in Christ shall not perish but have everlasting life." God loves all creation. Everything reflects God's energy of love and wise creativity. When we turn to the light and life of God, the Force of the Big Bang and the Inspiration of the prophets and Jesus is available to us. We receive the "power to become children of God" in the world of flesh, in our daily lives of body, mind, spirit, and relationships. We can transform the world for good and claim our vocation as God's companions in healing the world.

CONTEMPLATION

In this spiritual practice, take time once more to center yourself in stillness. Meditate on the affirmation "I have the power to become a child of God," asking yourself, "Where do I need God's power? Where can I embody God's power to heal the world? What situations in my life and relationships—in the world—need my power to heal and enlighten?" Let images and words emerge without judgment or editing. Following the pattern of spiritual visualization found in Meditation One, breathe in God's light, experiencing its healing and loving power. Breathe out Divine blessing on those situations that need your healing and loving power, experiencing your positive impact and ways you might be a messenger (an angel) of wholeness.

As you conclude, ask God to give you guidance to respond with love and light to the situations you visualized. Trust that God will enlighten and protect you in every encounter that calls upon your wisdom and love.

Power of the stars, sea, and sun,
empower me to join God's chorus of healing messengers.
Help me recognize the possibilities in life's limitations.
Give me insight to wisely bring light
and love to every encounter.
In the name of God's Child of Light. Amen.

MEDITATION THREE

AN IMPOSSIBLE POSSIBILITY

In the sixth month the angel Gabriel was sent by God to a town in Galilee called Nazareth, to a virgin engaged to a man whose name was Joseph, of the house of David. The virgin's name was Mary. And he came to her and said, "Greetings, favored one! Lord is with you." But she was much perplexed by his words and pondered what sort of greeting this might be. The angel said to her, "Do not be afraid, Mary, for you have found favor with God. And now, you will conceive in your womb and bear a son, and you will name him Jesus. He will be great and will be called the Son of the Most High, and the Lord God will give to him the throne of his ancestor David. He will reign over the house of Jacob forever, and of his kingdom there will be no end." Mary said to the angel, "How can this be, since I am a virgin?" The angel said to her, "The Holy Spirit will come upon you, and the power of the Most High will over-shadow you; therefore the child to be born will be holy; he will be called Son of God. And now, your relative Elizabeth in her old age has also conceived a son, and this is the sixth month for her who was said to be barren. For nothing will be impossible with God." Then Mary said, "Here am I, the servant of the Lord; let it be with me according to your word." Then the angel departed from her. (Luke 1:26–38)

All things reflect God's artistry and inspiration. The democracy of revelation embraces the Dalai Lama, Mother (Saint) Teresa, Alexandria Ocasio Cortes, Vladimir Putin, and Donald J. Trump. A young woman, Greta Thunberg, shall lead us, and the agony of parents whose children were massacred in American schools reflects the anger and anguish of God. There will come a time when all persons see God's light—experience God's enlightenment—and turn from our penchant for destruction to partner in God's new creation. That is the hope of Incarnation.

John's Gospel portrays revelation as ubiquitous and unquenchable. Like Elvis, God is everywhere. But some places—and people—are, as the Celtic spiritual guides assert, thin places and thin people, translucent in the light of Divine revelation, experiencing and revealing the very heart of God in their hearts. What is unique in the stories of Incarnation is the surprising reality that ordinary people, often unnoticed and marginalized, and persons of other religions all encounter the

Holy in ways that seem forbidden for religious and political leaders, as well as the rich and famous. God detours around Jerusalem, the home of the religious elite, to the little town of Bethlehem, a village of no consequence in the Roman Empire, and to a young girl without pedigree or profession. Shepherds hear the Hallelujah chorus, while Herod and the High Priest only hear the echoes of their own voices. God calls everyone. Often, though, we are so focused on our own agendas and perception of God's will, that we are unable to receive what God is revealing to us.

Mary of Nazareth is a young woman, perhaps, in early to mid-teens, recently betrothed to the carpenter Joseph. Although eventually she will have several children, the story suggests that she has not yet engaged in sexual relations when the angel Gabriel comes to visit. When an angel visits, everything is turned upside down for Mary. All her plans collapse, and a new and amazing future emerges.

Encountering the Life-Giver shakes up our lives. God refuses to be tucked safely away in a box. Ask Isaiah in the Temple who heard the angels cry "Holy, holy, holy is the LORD of hosts; the whole earth is full of his glory" (Isaiah 6:3). He cries in fear and awe, "Woe is me," and experiences the radical moral and spiritual distance between God and himself. Ask Jacob who wrestles with the Divine all night long, and rises in the morning with a limp, having met God and lived to tell the story. As Mr. Beaver in C.S. Lewis's *The Lion, Witch, and the Wardrobe* declares, in response to Lucy's query about whether or not Aslan is safe: "Safe?" said Mr. Beaver; "don't you hear what Mrs. Beaver tells you? Who said anything about safe? Course he isn't safe. But he's good. He's the King, I tell you. . . . He's wild you know. Not like a tame lion."

And when Gabriel visits with an amazing message, Mary is awestruck—but open-minded. She queries, "How can this be, since I am a virgin?" Gabriel's answer must have left her even more perplexed and amazed.

> "The Holy Spirit will come upon you, and the power of the Most High will overshadow you; therefore the child to be born will be holy; he will be called Son of God. And now, your relative Elizabeth in her old age has also conceived a son, and this is the sixth month for her who was said to be barren. For nothing will be impossible with God."

God presents her with an impossible possibility and Mary says "yes." On that "yes," God's vision of salvation depends. I think maybe the greatest miracle is that Mary says "yes." With all her wonder and perplexity, Mary responds,

"Here am I, the servant of the Lord; let it be with me according to your word."

Dag Hammarskjold (United Nations General Secretary from 1953–1961) describes the power of "yes" to transform us and the world:

> I don't know Who—or what—put the question, I don't know when it was put. I don't even remember answering. But at some moment I did answer Yes to Someone—or Something—and from that hour I was certain that existence is meaningful and that, therefore, my life in self-surrender, had a goal.[2]

We too are presented with impossible possibilities. Like Mary, we are also the womb and midwives of Divine revelation. We too are given opportunities to say "yes" to God. Mary is just like us. Her life is an icon, a window into the horizons of human hope and a mirror of what we can become when we say "yes" to God.

There is no need to invent doctrines to preserve Mary's sinlessness, protect her from sexually transmitted original sin, or exempt her from the realities of aging and death. Indeed, such doctrines focusing on Mary's purity either ethically or sexually render her not only irrelevant to our moral and spiritual lives but also devalue our own embodiment and sexuality.

We also don't need to worry about the obstetrical technicalities of Jesus' birth. Like the creation stories of Genesis, Jesus' conception cannot be explained scientifically or medically—nor can it be dismissed as fantasy. In a trillion-galaxy universe, the miraculous is always an option. In fact, as Walt Whitman notes, "All is miracle." However this conception occurs, God is at work in Mary's life, in her cells and her soul, and in the growth of the child to be. Spirit enlightens and enlivens her soul—and the cells of the newly conceived fetus.

Regardless of how you understand the conception of Jesus, it is essential to believe that Mary was conceived like every other child and that Jesus' siblings were conceived "the good old-fashioned way," through sexual intercourse. Apart from such an affirmation, sexuality becomes a necessary evil and sinful, rather than an act of human love, creativity, and joyful embodiment. The heavens declare the glory of God—and so does the loving conception of each child. The Incarnation declares that God acts in and through our bodies, and that no aspect of human life is off limits for Divine revelation

John the Baptist's prenatal gymnastics punctuate this story. The child of another unexpected and unplanned pregnancy—that of aged Zechariah and the post-menopausal

Elizabeth—John rejoices from the womb. There is a spiritual synchronicity between John and Jesus that lasts for a lifetime. Medical studies—and mothers' wisdom—tell us that fetuses are aware of their physical and emotional environment. They can hear music in the womb and then recognize it later as infants and toddlers. The graceful and dynamic interdependence of life embraces all creation, from conception to everlasting life. John prenatally "knows" Jesus. When he experiences the "thin place," the marriage of Infinite and intimate that joins Jesus and himself, he leaps for joy! The spiritual lives of mothers and families—and the impact of the environment—shapes life in the womb and is the *in-utero* foundation for a child's future. The reality of prenatal experience and responsiveness to environmental influences clearly have ethical implications. Not only does it suggest that fetuses—along with their mothers—deserve ethical consideration, but it also mandates that institutions support the quality of life of pregnant women, parents, and families; just economics; loving environments; and adequate fetal health care. Every fetus carried to term and then welcomed at birth deserves a healthy and loving prenatal environment and a period of gestation characterized by good nutrition, stability, and community support.

The future depends upon Mary's great "yes." Let us also seek to embrace the path of Mary and love this good Earth.

When we are called, may we respond with freedom and creativity, "Here am I, the servant of the Lord; let it be with me according to your word."

CONTEMPLATION

After a time of quiet reflection, prayerfully read Howard Thurman's "Growing Edge," letting its words soak in and take root in your spirit.

> Look well to the growing edge! All around us worlds are dying, and new worlds are being born; all around us life is dying, and life is being born. . . . This is the basis of hope in moments of despair, the incentive to carry on when times are out of joint and men have lost their reason, the source of confidence when worlds crash and dreams whiten into ash. The birth of the child—life's most dramatic answer to death—this is the growing edge incarnate. Look well to the growing edge![3]

If you are able, go on a prayer walk, letting insights and inspirations flow with each step. Return home reflecting on the question, "What is the growing edge in my life and how can I embody it?"

Our prayers find their completion in practice, and our contemplation is fulfilled in commitment to creative transformation of ourselves and the world. Let the affirmation of Mary's "yes" to Jesus' birth inspire you to greater care for mothers, families, and children, not just those of your immediate community or nation, but globally, through acts of personal kindness and generosity and advocacy for children's health and rights, most especially the rights of immigrant and refugee children such as Jesus of Nazareth. Prayerfully reflect on where you are called to embrace God's great "yes" in your life. How will you discover and nurture the great "yes" toward which God is calling you?

God of every tomorrow,
inspire us toward your new horizons of loving service.
Help us recognize and nurture
your great "yes" in our lives.
Help us nurture the Christ-child being born in us.
Let us make a home for every new life
and create a world in which every child
is welcomed, affirmed, loved,
and given the opportunity to live an abundant life.
And let us sing with God's people
from all times and places, and the whole Earth:

O Holy Child of Bethlehem,

Descend to us, we pray.

Cast out our sin and enter in,

Be born in us today.

We hear the Christmas angels

The great glad tidings tell,

O come to us, abide with us,

Our Lord Emmanuel.

In the Name and Spirit of the Christ-Child. Amen.

AN UNLIKELY REVOLUTIONARY

My soul magnifies the Lord, my spirit rejoices in God my
Savior, for he has looked with favor on the lowliness of his
servant. Surely, from now on all generations will call me
blessed; for the Mighty One has done great things for me,
and holy is his name. His mercy is for those who fear him
from generation to generation. He has shown strength
with his arm; he has scattered the proud in the thoughts
of their hearts. He has brought down the powerful from
their thrones, and lifted up the lowly; he has filled the
hungry with good things, and sent the rich away empty.
(Luke 1:46–53)

An unmarried, pregnant teenager becomes a prophet.
An unlettered young woman channels the spirits of
Amos and Micah, Isaiah, and Jeremiah. While many scholars
doubt the veracity of Mary's proclamation, noting that these

words are likely a later addition and couldn't have come from a woman with Mary's level of education and social and economic status, the fact that these words are attributed to Mary of Nazareth should fill us with amazement and challenge our assumptions about the relationship between Divine inspiration and gender, economics, and education. If a little child can lead humankind, so can a working-class teenager!

Luke's Pentecost theology proclaims the universality of revelation, cutting across the artificial and unjust divisions that characterize human experience:

> In the last days it will be, God declares, that I will pour out my Spirit upon all flesh, and your sons and your daughters shall prophesy, and your young men shall see visions, and your old men shall dream dreams. Even upon my slaves, both men and women, in those days I will pour out my Spirit, and they shall prophesy. (Acts 2:17–18)

Fifteen-year-old Greta Thunberg, diagnosed as being on the autism spectrum, can initiate strikes to combat climate change and shame the world's leaders. Twenty-two-year-old Amanda Gorman can give the Inaugural Poem and challenge adults and children alike to embrace the light of freedom and justice in words echoing Jesus' affirmation in Matthew 5: "If only we're brave enough to see it, if only we're brave enough to be it." Another teenager, Mary of Nazareth, can speak God's word for her time and place, embracing the message of the prophets for her time and ours.

Mary's words challenge any Christian perspective that denies the connection between spirituality and politics. She is speaking to individuals, but she is also challenging the structures that perpetuate poverty and injustice. As an oppressed, economically vulnerable person, Mary knows the impact of political and economic decisions, whether made in Jerusalem or Rome. She knows that all politics and economics are personal. Decisions made in palaces and counting houses can make the difference between survival and starvation for the poor of the land. To God, everything is personal. As Abraham Joshua Heschel says, the Divine pathos, God's empathy with humankind and creation, means that what happens in the marketplace happens to God.[4] God not only hears the cries of the poor and powerless; God also feels their pain as God's own pain. God is "the fellow sufferer who understands." What happens to "the least of these" shapes God's experience. Legislative inability and recalcitrance to protect school children from gun violence and provide resources for young mothers touch the heart of God, evoking prophetic indignation.

Mary doesn't mince words in the Magnificat! She has the bluntness of Amos and the incisiveness of Micah. Justice must "roll down like waters, and righteousness like an ever-flowing stream" (Amos 5:24). Unless they change their ways, the wealthy and powerful will be sent home empty-handed, crushed by the weight of their own possessions. The poor and vulnerable, the trod-upon salt of the earth, will feast at God's smorgasbord and their children will go to the best schools. The schemes and machinations of the powerful and wealthy will come to nothing, crushed by the inexorable movements of the moral arc of history. The poor people of the earth will not only march, companioned by Martin Luther King and William Barber; they will skip and dance, leap and pirouette, delighting in the emergence of God's realm of Shalom.

Mary did not live to see her vision come to fruition. We are still waiting. But we must not give up hope. Mary's words challenge and lure. Her song joining God's glory and social justice convicts us of our hopelessness and apathy, "our weak resignation to the evils we deplore," and invites us to be vanguards of God's green and graceful new deal, to repair the world, and claim our vocations as God's companions in Shalom.

Mary's message is contagious. The melodious mysticism of a teenager evokes prophetic utterance from the elder

Zechariah. In speaking of his son's role in preparing the way for the Most High, the One who will transform the world, Zechariah joins the chorus:

> Because of the tender mercy of our God, the dawn from on high will break upon us, to shine upon those who sit in darkness and in the shadow of death, to guide our feet into the way of peace. (Luke 1:78–79)

From the fecund darkness of Elizabeth's and Mary's wombs the prophet Isaiah's message of hope for the oppressed and broken, the hard-hearted and sinful, will burst forth:

> The people who walked in darkness have seen a great light; those who lived in a land of deep darkness—on them light has shined. (Isaiah 9:2)

And in response, we "arise, shine, for our light has come, and the glory of the Lord has risen upon us" (Isaiah 60:1, my paraphrase).

I need to confess that I am more inclined to the life of professor, pastor, and contemplative than activist or prophet. Yet I must also assert that the times cry out for justice seekers, peacemakers, and prophetic healers whose mystical experiences drive them to mission. African American mystic and spiritual guide Howard Thurman, whose work influenced Martin Luther King, Jesse Jackson, Bayard Rustin, and other civil rights leaders, recognized that the mystic is challenged to confront everything that stands in the way of persons achieving their full humanity.

Mary of Nazareth was an unintentional activist. She was a woman in a patriarchal society and had little voice outside the confines of her household. She was also of low estate, likely uneducated and untrained in the ways of politics. Yet, Matthew envisions Mary as a world-shaker and world-shaper. She challenges the status quo and invites us to challenge injustice, using our gifts to heal the spirit and economics of our nation and the planet.

CONTEMPLATION

In the spirit of Mary of Nazareth, I invite you to incarnate her words through an updated practice of Lectio Divina, or holy reading, an imaginative approach to scripture that joins heart, hands, and head. Take time to read silently Mary's Magnificat (Luke 1:46–53), letting the words soak in. After a few minutes of silence, read the scripture again, prayerfully and deliberately experiencing any insights as they wash over your thoughts and emotions. Following the second reading, take ten minutes, and weather and health permitting, embark on a prayer walk, listening to God's message in the words of scripture. If a particular word, image, or phrase emerges, dwell on this insight. Ask for God's guidance to discern its meaning in your life. Conclude by giving thanks for your insights and asking for God's wisdom in embodying them in daily life and, possibly, political or institutional involvement. Stay with your insights throughout the day, training your attention for invitations to commitment you may receive through chance encounters or headline news.

Mary of Nazareth, mother of Jesus,

whose love makes way for Divine revelation,

enlighten our path and guide our ways

that we might go from self-interest to world loyalty.

Let us be mothers and midwives

of Holy Adventure and New Creation,

life-givers in a world enamored of death.

Fill us with the Divine Energy

that makes seedlings sprout

from the ashes of destruction. Amen.

ANCESTRY MATTERS

An account of the genealogy of Jesus the Messiah, the son of David, the son of Abraham. Abraham was the father of Isaac, and Isaac the father of Jacob, and Jacob the father of Judah and his brothers, and Judah the father of Perez and Zerah by Tamar, and Perez the father of Hezron, and Hezron the father of Aram, and Aram the father of Aminadab, and Aminadab the father of Nahshon, and Nahshon the father of Salmon, and Salmon the father of Boaz by Rahab, and Boaz the father of Obed by Ruth, and Obed the father of Jesse, and Jesse the father of King David. And David was the father of Solomon by the wife of Uriah, and Solomon the father of Rehoboam, and Rehoboam the father of Abijah, and Abijah the father of Asaph, and Asaph the father of Jehoshaphat, and Jehoshaphat the father of Joram, and Joram the father of Uzziah, and Uzziah the father of Jotham, and Jotham the father of Ahaz, and Ahaz the father of Hezekiah, and Hezekiah the father of Manasseh, and Manasseh the father of Amos, and Amos the father of Josiah, and Josiah the father of Jechoniah and his brothers, at the time of the deportation to Babylon. And after the deportation to Babylon: Jechoniah was the father of Salathiel, and Salathiel the father of Zerubbabel, and Zerubbabel the father of Abiud, and Abiud the father of Eliakim, and Eliakim the father of Azor, and Azor the father of Zadok, and Zadok the father of Achim, and Achim the father of Eliud, and Eliud the father of Eleazar, and Eleazar the father of Matthan, and Matthan the father of Jacob, and Jacob the father of Joseph the husband of Mary, who bore Jesus, who is called the Messiah. (Matthew 1:1–15)

I n one way or another, most of us are curious about our roots and the interconnections we have with contemporary relatives about whom we have no knowledge. On *Finding Your Roots,* Henry Louis Gates Jr. traces the ancestry of celebrities and political leaders, captivating both the subjects of his studies and his television viewers. Many of us are members of Ancestry.com, and, in the process of studying our family tree, we discover new friends and family members, learning more about our origins than we had previously imagined. We need both roots and wings, a sense of history in its concreteness that gives birth to novel possibilities.

Matthew claims to chart Jesus' lineage to forty-two generations. This tracing is imaginative rather than historically accurate. In fact, a close reading of Matthew reveals that he names only forty generations. Matthew affirms, however, that Jesus is rooted in the history of Israel, its great and the near great, successes and failures, and kings and farmers. In effect, Matthew is telling us, "This is where Jesus came from."[5]

Plato begins his dialogue on theology, spirituality, and rhetoric, the *Phaedrus,* with wise Socrates inquiring of youthful Phaedrus, "Where have you come from and where are you going?" The young man initially assumes the question demands a factual response and gives a report of his day thus far and his plans for the afternoon and evening. The wise philosopher's questions are much more probing than Phaedrus assumes, however. Socrates is asking the youth to shift his attention from the everyday to the eternal and reflect on his cosmic origins and the spiritual destiny that lies before him. We come to earth, "trailing clouds of glory," as the poet William Wordsworth notes, but all too soon forget our Divine origins, identity, and destiny.

The philosopher Alfred North Whitehead writes that the whole universe conspires to create each moment of experience. While the exact details of the future cannot be determined, the past is prologue and catalyst of our present and future decisions as persons and nations. We cannot escape the impact of past personal and corporate decisions. They have an immortality with which we must contend even when we attempt to transform and heal our past mistakes and injustices.

The United States debates about whether the history of slavery and the genocide of the First Americans should be taught in schools. For some people, recalling the United States' ambiguous history is a threat to the self-esteem of white children and will eventually lead to replacing white privilege with Black power. To other persons, the truth about American history in all its tragedy and historical ambiguity will enable us to make just decisions today, embracing all of us, in the future. In truth, personal and national healing is possible only if we confront with honesty the achievements and errors of our past, the traumas and moments of redemption, and the limits and possibilities inherited from our family of origin and founding parents.

I believe Matthew would side with those who teach Critical Race Theory, reminding us that healing the soul of the nation can occur only when we claim the totality of our history and not just our achievements and successes. Matthew knows that the Messiah can be known fully only if we embrace the totality of human history, the history of Israel, and the current political situation of occupation and oppression.

The Word and Wisdom of God is the motivating power behind the historical process, seeking to move the moral and spiritual arcs of history forward, despite human waywardness and conceit. God's incarnation is always embodied in the concreteness of politics, economics, and family life. As Psalm 8 affirms, what we do matters to ourselves, future generations, the unfolding of Earth's history, and God. Human history is the interplay of Divine call and human response, and Divine inspiration and human agency.

Jesus the Messiah is not a historical outsider but at the heart of history. The flesh-and-blood Messiah, the Child of Bethlehem, grew to be the world's Savior. For Matthew, Jesus' birth is naturalistic in nature and begins with the "father" of the Hebrew people, Abraham. Luke's genealogy, located in his text following Jesus' baptism by John the Baptist, begins with Jesus, the goal of human history, and reaches back to Adam, the "parent" of humankind. Jesus' historical, ethnic, and political location matters. Jesus' physical existence, not just his spirituality matters. Not the product of a supernaturalistic rescue operation, defying the causal structure of the universe, Jesus is the spiritual fullness of what nature can be, fully human, fully Divine, and fully alive.

Many years ago, a retired school administrator and a member of one of my Bible study groups, raised the question,

"What about the women? Where do they fit in God's revelation?" Matthew's genealogy provides a positive, though controversial, response to my congregant's question. Matthew focuses on five women: Tamar, Rahab, Ruth, the unnamed Bathsheba, and Mary as ancestors of Jesus. Four of them color outside the lines, violate the norms of their society, and embark on adventures to secure the well-being of themselves, their families, and the world. Tamar tricks her father-in-law into sleeping with her to ensure the continuation of her husband's lineage. Rahab is a Canaanite sex worker, who chooses to be loyal to the children of Israel rather than her native Jericho. Ruth is a Moabite widow, another ethnic outsider, who lures Boaz into an intimate relationship to ensure the survival of her mother-in-law Naomi and herself. Out of Ruth and Boaz's marriage, the line of Israel's greatest king David is established. Mary of Nazareth encounters an angel and gives birth to God's Beloved Son, despite the possibility of disgrace and death. Each one is a social and religious outsider for whom the circumstances of life, and God's movements in their lives, call them to do what had previously been impossible and unthinkable. In a world in which women always deferred to their male counterparts, be they husbands, brothers, or fathers, each of these four women takes control of their destiny. They become, like Queen Esther, world-shapers, whose calling is to further God's vision "for just such a time as this" (see Esther 4:14).

The fifth woman, referred to as the "wife of Uriah," cannot say "no" to King David's advances. He has power and as a woman and wife of one of David's subordinates, she is powerless. There is no romance, only male lust and domination, in this relationship. When she becomes pregnant, David has her husband assigned to the battlefront, where he is killed. Upon Uriah's death, David takes Bathsheba into the palace to be his wife. Finding her own power, Bathsheba, with the support of the prophet Nathan, successfully conspires to have her son succeed David as King of Israel. Bathsheba is a moral outsider, whose initiative makes her, like the other four, an actor on the stage of history, and not a victim, of David's sexual misconduct.

Why did Matthew choose *these* women to mention? Perhaps to show us that as the descendent of these five women, Jesus is deeply rooted in the moral and spiritual tensions of life. Without the agency of two sexually assertive women, a sex worker, a victim who found her political voice, and an angelic pregnancy, Jesus would not have been born! Jesus has ethical skeletons in his closet, including the sexual escapades of David and Solomon!

Ancestry matters! Regardless of his heavenly origins, Jesus is the child of the Earth. He has our human DNA and the DNA of all Earth creatures. His salvation is of the Earth, by the Earth, and for the Earth, lived out in the history of imaginative and soulful human beings in all their wondrous embodiment. The Gospel genealogies remind us that salvation occurs in the scrum of history, politics, economics, and embodiment. God heals the world by being in the world, and the Divine Healer challenges us to play our role in healing the Earth.

Dag Hammarskjold prayed: "For all that has been—thanks! For all that shall be—yes!"[6] This quote has appeared someplace in virtually every book I've written over the past two decades, for it reflects what I believe to be the heart of a responsible spirituality. Gratitude leads to gracefulness. Thanksgiving inspires agency. Claiming the best of the past aims us toward future possibilities.

CONTEMPLATION

In this spiritual practice, I invite you to reflect imaginatively on your ancestors, beginning with your biological and spiritual parents and grandparents, mentors, teachers, siblings, giving thanks for their positive impact on your life. Then reach back as far as you can in your family tree to your biological and spiritual predecessors, again, giving thanks for their positive influence on your life. You may not know them, and they may have been ethically and relationally ambiguous, but you are here now because of who they were. Next, visualize the human adventure that has led to this point in your life, remembering the gifts of those who first looked at the heavens in wonder, invented the wheel, developed language and symbolism, created medicine, and soared to the heavens in mystical experiences. Visualize with gratitude the world-changing spiritual teachers—patriarchs and matriarchs, monastics and shamans, healers and spiritual teachers such as Amos, Jesus, Buddha, Lao Tzu, Black Elk, and Starhawk. Give thanks for them and those persons whose teachings and writings have shaped you. Give thanks for the human adventure that gave birth to your spiritual adventures.

From gratitude comes the great "yes." Set aside time to prayerfully reflect on God's great "yes" in your life. Where are the contours of graceful gratitude leading you? What new possibilities lure your forward? Where is God calling you?

Finally, set aside time to ask the question, "How can I be a good ancestor to my children and grandchildren, to the generations that lie ahead, most of whom I will never meet? How can I do something beautiful for those who will succeed me on the Earth adventure?" Let your reflections inspire commitment to healing today's crises, such as climate change, racism, gun violence, or economic injustice. Let your circles of care go beyond yourself to embrace the whole Earth.

Thank you, Life-Giver,
for the deeply woven roots of life.
Thank you for those who have been my parents,
mentors, kin, siblings, and companions.
Thank you for the good Earth from which I come.
Let me be known as a good ancestor
to those who follow me,
one who loves the Earth and protects all life.
In Jesus' name. Amen

LIVING THE DREAM

Now the birth of Jesus the Messiah took place in this way. When his mother Mary had been engaged to Joseph, but before they lived together, she was found to be pregnant from the Holy Spirit. Her husband Joseph, being a righteous man and unwilling to expose her to public disgrace, planned to divorce her quietly. But just when he had resolved to do this, an angel of the Lord appeared to him in a dream and said, "Joseph, son of David, do not be afraid to take Mary as your wife, for the child conceived in her is from the Holy Spirit. She will bear a son, and you are to name him Jesus, for he will save his people from their sins." All this took place to fulfill what had been spoken by the Lord through the prophet: "Look, the virgin shall become pregnant and give birth to a son, and they shall name him Emmanuel, which means, "God is with us."

When Joseph awoke from sleep, he did as the angel of the Lord commanded him; he took her as his wife but had no marital relations with her until she had given birth to a son, and he named him Jesus. (Matthew 1:18–25)

G od communicates to humankind in a variety of ways. A still, small voice. A strangely warmed heart. An unexpected encounter. A vision. An intuition. A sunset or starry, starry night. A grandchild's face or an immigrant's fears. An omnipresent, omni-active God influences each moment of experience. We are always on holy ground, and sometimes we, like Jacob after his dream of a ladder of angels, stammer in amazement, "Surely God was in this place—and I did not know it!" (see Genesis 28:10–22). Every place is Beth-El, the gateway to Divinity for those whose doors of perception have been cleansed and opened.

God addresses us in conscious deliberations—theological reflection, spiritual counsel, ethical decision-making—and unconsciously in dreams and intuitions. Dreams figure prominently in the stories of Jesus' birth and infancy. Joseph the father of Jesus, like his historical namesake, is the recipient of several life-changing dreams: counsel to marry his pregnant fiancé Mary (Matthew 1:18–25), save the infant Jesus and his family by fleeing to Egypt (Matthew 2:13), return home with his family following Herod's death (Matthew 2:19–21), and settle his family in Nazareth (Matthew 2:22–23).

Uncertain about how to respond to Mary's pregnancy, Joseph receives an angelic visitation in a dream, telling him not to be afraid, just as the angel reassured Elizabeth and

Zechariah in their unexpected pregnancy. The angel charged Joseph to marry his fiancé despite the potentially negative impact on his reputation and tells him to name this unexpected child "Jesus," the one who will save his people from their sins.

Coming from a religious community that takes dreams seriously as media of Divine revelation, Joseph follows the angel's counsel; he marries the pregnant Mary and commits to parenting their son Jesus. In the process, he saves Mary from disgrace and perhaps death, and he provides a home and spiritual foundation for the child Jesus.

While Mary's virginity is the source of Joseph's perplexity, once again, the point of the angelic message to Joseph is not ultimately obstetrics but Joseph's fidelity to God. The nature and circumstances of Jesus' conception will always remain a mystery. While contemporary scholars have speculated that Mary's pregnancy was the result of rape by a Roman soldier, there is no documentary evidence for this assertion. To be honest, I have never concerned myself with Jesus' origins: whether Jesus' origins relate to wanted or forced sexual intercourse or the miracles of Divine companionship, Mary's pregnancy was miraculous. God was present with Mary at Jesus' conception and throughout her life, even though she was, at times, anxious about her son's spiritual independence and the risks he was taking with his gospel of God's realm of inclusive healing and hospitality. And regardless of the cause of Mary's pregnancy, Divine or human, Joseph is an essential part of the story: Joseph also says "yes" to God, protecting Mary from death or disgrace and ensuring that Jesus is born into a stable (as well as in a stable!) and loving family.

Joseph's uniqueness is his willingness to love a child whose paternity was in question. His love for Mary and his obedience to God supersedes any misgivings or reputational concerns on his part. Joseph says "yes" with all his doubts. Joseph's great "yes" inspires us to consider the great "yeses" to which God invites us: opportunities to embody impossible possibilities, to play our part in bringing beauty and justice to the world. Joseph also reminds us, as theologian Paul Tillich asserts, that living faith includes doubt as well as certainty, and that our doubts may open us to wisdom in understanding God's presence in the world and our lives.

CONTEMPLATION

Dreams can be a source of inspiration, creativity, and revelation. If God is omnipresent and omni-active, then God must be moving in our sleep as well as our waking hours. God is still speaking, whispering in "sighs too deep for words," and if we listen, we may hear the Spirit's messages for us and to the world. Accordingly, John Sanford is correct in describing dreams as "God's forgotten language."[7]

For many years, I have employed the following practice to enhance my creativity, especially when I am writing. Before I go to sleep, I briefly take a few minutes to reflect on my current writing project. I either write a brief note or read some of the notes I've been working on or simply mull over what I will write about the next day. I consciously open to Divine inspiration and ask that God be at work in my unconscious while I am sleeping. When I awaken each morning, I begin the day with a time of contemplation. Then, armed with a cup of strong coffee, I start writing, trusting that my unconscious has been ruminating throughout the night and that I will receive some of the insights I experienced nocturnally.

Another practice to deepen your awareness of God's movements in dreams and synchronous encounters is to ask for Divine healing or inspiration while you are sleeping. Trusting Jesus' promise, "Ask and you shall receive," the process of asking prepares you to remember any insightful or healing dreams you receive. When you wake up, immediately jot down anything you remember from your dreams. You may want to create a dream journal specifically for recording and reflecting on your dreams.

Many persons receive significant insights related to important decisions or spiritual questions from paying attention to dreams. Often people receive a greater understanding of a specific life issue or problem they are seeking to resolve. God's promise of abundant life includes the totality of our lives, body, mind, spirit, and relationships—and even our dreams.

God of insight and inspiration,
God of sleeping and waking,
speak to me in my dreams as well as my deliberations
Grant me insight
and the wisdom and courage to act on my insights
to bring wholeness to my life
and well-being to those around me. Amen

EMBEDDED IN HISTORY

In those days a decree went out from Caesar Augustus that all the world should be registered. This was the first registration and was taken while Quirinius was governor of Syria. All went to their own towns to be registered. Joseph also went from the town of Nazareth in Galilee to Judea, to the city of David called Bethlehem, because he was descended from the house and family of David. He went to be registered with Mary, to whom he was engaged and who was expecting a child. While they were there, the time came for her to deliver her child. And she gave birth to her firstborn son and wrapped him in bands of cloth and laid him in a manger, because there was no place in the guest room. (Luke 2:1–7)

Luke's account of Jesus' birth begins with a historical observation: "In those days a decree went out from Caesar Augustus." While John's Gospel roots Jesus' birth in the cosmos, and Matthew sees Jesus as at the heart of Jewish history, descended from royalty and women of agency and adventure, Luke places Jesus in the scrum of first-century history, embedded in the politics of Roman occupation and Jewish restlessness. Luke stresses that Jesus was born in a particular time and place, and a political, historical, and cultural context.

Quirinius was listed as governor of Syria, although scholars believe he began his gubernatorial term in 6 CE, almost ten years after Jesus' birth. This discrepancy is curious since knowledge of the years of Quirinius' leadership would have been available to the author of Luke's Gospel. It's possible that Quirinius had an earlier term as governor, but in any case, while history is important to the Gospel writers, the *meaning* of history is more significant than exact dating.

Luke is making clear that Jesus was born in an occupied land, with all the tension and oppression that entailed.

The Nation of Israel during Jesus' day was much like today's Palestine. Although Jews, like Palestinians today, had a proud history, they could no longer determine their political destiny and were at the mercy of faraway rulers, as well as the day-to-day indignities and violence of the occupying troops. Jesus and his contemporaries lived under the threat of violence and humiliation that could be exercised by the occupying forces at any moment. Resentment was high, and historical restlessness at a fever pitch. The dream of a political Messiah, who would overturn Roman rule and exile traitors like Herod, energized hope for the future, even as it also generated violence among guerrilla bands such as the Zealots.

Luke's short introduction to Jesus' birth reveals a truth that can only be appreciated by peoples subjugated by foreign or domestic powers: Uyghurs in China, residents of Gaza and Palestine, and African Americans in the era of Jim Crow restrictions and lynching, as well as today's "kinder and gentler" James Crow, revealed in voting-rights restrictions and unequal policing practices.

Jesus never spent a moment of his life as a politically free person. He was always at the political and legal mercy of the Roman occupying forces and their Jewish representatives. He had no legal rights and could be impressed into service, carrying a Roman soldier's equipment and luggage a mile or surrendering his cloak merely on a whim.

Divine incarnation takes place in the uncertainties and inconveniences of history, among people who would have been barely noticed or seen as inferior and unimportant by those holding the levers of political and economic power. At best, Joseph and his family were "human resources," individually replaceable but corporately necessary to support the ambitions of the Roman Empire. At worst, they were potential revolutionaries, who must be held in check to maintain law and order, while keeping steady the stream of money to Rome and its Jewish surrogates.

As working-class people, Mary and Joseph had to depend on luck and the kindness of strangers in their quest for lodging. We don't know the exact details of their dwelling place, but we can suspect a cave or stable or an open room adjoining a courtyard, where domestic animals normally were kept. These ordinary beasts were probably present at Jesus' birth.

The description of Jesus' birth is simple and understated: "And she gave birth to her firstborn son and wrapped him in bands of cloth and laid him in a manger, because there was no place in the guest room." Did Mary and Joseph go from house to house and inn to inn (inns were likely no more than houses with an extra room or two for lodging), as the festival of Las Posadas depicts? How many people turned them down, before one innkeeper or householder invited them to sleep with the family's domestic animals?

We don't know if the timing of Jesus' birth was anticipated by Mary and Joseph. Did Joseph have any leeway in terms of travel to Bethlehem or was a particular date demanded, regardless of Mary's condition? Did the discomfort of the journey cause Mary to go into labor prematurely?

All we know is that Jesus was born in the humblest of environments. While there is beauty in childbirth, and every child bears the face of God, a manger is no place to put a baby. Mangers are feeding boxes or troughs for cattle, pigs, and sheep. The environment of Jesus' birth reveals his parents' economic status. More important, it reveals God's incarnation in the "least of these," those easily overlooked and mistreated by the powerful and privileged. God shows up anywhere. God has no reservations about revealing Godself in refugees stranded on the U.S.-Mexico border; in an impoverished family living from paycheck to paycheck; in a young couple, in recovery from addiction, struggling to stay sober as they prepare for the birth of their first child; or in a gay or lesbian couple dealing with prejudice from the Christian moral police as they go through adoption procedures.

What is miraculous about the Incarnation is its utter messiness, ordinariness, and unpretentiousness. Embedded in history, economics, and politics, God is born among us. Incarnation embraces the nuisances and nobodies, as John Dominic Crossan avers,[8] as well as the chaos of our own lives.

We too can experience God in all of God's distressing and surprising disguises, whether among undocumented "essential" farm workers, sex workers in the shadows of urban areas, on the golf course at Mar-al-Lago, or in our own complicated and ambiguous lives. When we see God's light in the least of these, the whole Earth becomes a place of beauty, and God's glory shines in us and all things, inviting us to become lights in the world, sharing the grace we have received.

While it is often the case that religion and politics don't mix well, and that people use religion to prop up their own prejudice and persecute those who differ from themselves, authentic spirituality shines a light on economics and politics, challenging us, in the spirit of Abraham Lincoln, to follow the better angels of our nature. The spirituality of the prophets inspired Martin Luther King to seek justice and equality. The Sermon on the Mount was a polestar for Mahatma Gandhi in the practice of *ahimsa* and *satyagraha,* nonviolent resistance and civil disobedience, to secure his country's freedom from British rule. God's care for the least of these motivates the Poor People's March and the quest to end gun violence in the United States. Truly, the personal is the political, and the political is the personal. Jesus' followers are called to "let justice roll down like waters, and righteousness like an ever-flowing stream" (Amos 5:24). In his own inaugural message, Jesus joined the Divine and historical in quoting the prophet Isaiah as his mission statement:

The Spirit of the Lord is upon me, because he has anointed me to bring good news to the poor. He has sent me to proclaim release to the captives and recovery of sight to the blind, to set free those who are oppressed, to proclaim the year of the Lord's favor. (Luke 4:18–19)

CONTEMPLATION

Given Jesus' vision of prophetic healing that joins personal and social transformation, prayerfully consider God's calling for you in our own historical moment. You may not be called to be a public figure or activist, but you can challenge the powers and principalities in other ways.

In a time of prayerful reflection, perhaps over a several-day period, ask God, "What is your calling for me in this time of place?" God's vocation comes to us in the midst of history, and the circumstances of our personal lives and citizenship. Ask God to open your eyes to the poor and vulnerable, and your ears to hear their cries. Ask God to break your heart as you move from apathy to empathy and then to action. Each step on the way, walk prayerfully and lovingly, even with those who perpetrate injustice.

Holy One, guide my steps

that I might walk in your light.

Open my heart

that I might feel the pain

of the vulnerable and marginalized.

Open my mind

to learn about injustice and violence in our world.

Open my hands

that I might be an instrument

of your grace and peace,

your partner in healing the world.

In the name of the Child, Jesus. Amen.

NUISANCES AND NOBODIES

Now in that same region there were shepherds living in the fields, keeping watch over their flock by night. Then an angel of the Lord stood before them, and the glory of the Lord shone around them, and they were terrified. But the angel said to them, "Do not be afraid, for see, I am bringing you good news of great joy for all the people: to you is born this day in the city of David a Savior, who is the Messiah, the Lord. This will be a sign for you: you will find a child wrapped in bands of cloth and lying in a manger." And suddenly there was with the angel a multitude of the heavenly host, praising God and saying, "Glory to God in the highest heaven, and on earth peace among those whom he favors!"

When the angels had left them and gone into heaven, the shepherds said to one another, "Let us go now to Bethlehem and see this thing that has taken place, which the Lord has made known to us." So they went with haste and found Mary and Joseph and the child lying in the manger. When they saw this, they made known what had been told them about this child, and all who heard it were amazed at what the shepherds told them, and Mary treasured all these words and pondered them in her heart. The shepherds returned, glorifying and praising God for all they had heard and seen, just as it had been told them. (Luke 2:8–20)

John Dominic Crossan describes Jesus' community as a kingdom of nuisances and nobodies,[9] people at the edges of society, without economic and political power, and often marginalized, excluded, or looked down upon by the economic and religious elite. Those who were neglected by the rich and famous, the power-hungry and pompous, were the apple of God's eye and the object of Jesus' love.

As I've noted throughout our meditations, God's incarnation in Jesus the Christ occurs precisely among society's and religion's outsiders. Mary and Joseph were of no account to the movers and shakers of Rome and Jerusalem. They didn't even matter as pilgrims to backwater Bethlehem. But, at the margins, among the oppressed and powerless, God creates a "thin place" in which heaven and earth are joined and the forgotten and ostracized discover their divinity. When we awaken to God's inspiration, margins can become the frontiers, birthing a new world.

Despite the romantic visions of our Christmas pageants, the shepherds who received God's angelic visitation were at the lower rungs of society. Like many of today's "essential" workers, shepherds were a dime a dozen, easily replaceable, and without portfolio or status. Luke accentuates the shepherds' lowly status by noting that they were "living in the fields, keeping watch over their flock by night." Were they houseless, just making enough to get by and not able to purchase a permanent dwelling, or were they so overworked that they seldom had time to be with their families? Could they have been like the 140 million American families who live from paycheck to paycheck, having to work two jobs to put food on the table, and provide shelter for their families, with little time for relaxation or recreation with their loved ones?

In the first century, shepherds were among the peasant class, often looked down up by persons of financial substance. They were the objects of judgment, suspicion, and ridicule. Given religious and cultural beliefs, then and now, that a person's economic status reflects their morality and ambition, shepherds were seen, as many of the poor are today, as lazy and shiftless. In polite society, shepherds were considered shady and not to be trusted. They were smelly and dirty, like the flocks they tended.[10] Yet this is precisely where the fullness of revelation occurs. This is where the songs of the Hallelujah chorus break from among angelic hosts.

When the angels appear, the shepherds are gobsmacked. The brightness of the angelic visitor amazes them, and perhaps they wonder, "What is an angel doing among us? What have we done, good or bad, to deserve an angelic visitation?" Intuiting their consternation, the angel comforts them: "Do not be afraid, for see, I am bringing you good news of great joy for all the people: to you is born this day in the city of David a Savior, who is the Messiah, the Lord. This will be a sign for you: you will find a child wrapped in bands of cloth and lying in a manger."

Today's popular spirituality sees angels as comforting and innocuous. In contrast, in the biblical tradition, recipients of angelic visitations are consistently terrified. Just as the angel counseled Mary and Joseph, the angel of God assures the shepherds: "Don't be afraid. All will be well. My visit will bless you. I have a message for you, for good and not evil, for a hopeful future. Follow me, and you will be astounded and forever changed."

In the wake of the angel's counsel, all heaven breaks loose. The whole Earth is filled with God's glory as the angels burst forth in praise: "Glory to God in the highest heaven!"

This Child will bring peace to the Earth. Not the peace that comes from law and order, violence and oppression, the peace of the emperor Augustus Caesar, but a very different kind of peace, the peace that comes from justice and equity, the peace of the Divine ruler, the Messiah, Jesus the Christ. The Christ Child will transform the world through relational and economic healing, through nonviolent spiritual and communal transformation; he is not the violent Messiah imagined by Jewish zealots, the mirror image of Caesar, who will destroy the Romans to secure the freedom of Israel.

Amazed by their angelic visitors, all the shepherds can do in response is follow the angelic counsel and go to Bethlehem, to worship and praise. There, they are transformed by God's glory, lying in a humble manger. We don't know what happened to the shepherds after they returned to their flocks. I suspect that they were forever changed.

In describing the angelic visitation to the shepherds, Howard Thurman notes that we all need to hear the songs of angels:

> There must be always remaining in every [person's] life some place for the singing of the angels—some-place for that which in itself is breathlessly beautiful and by an inherent prerogative throwing all the rest of

life into a new and created relatedness. . . . The commonplace is shot through now with new glory—old burdens become lighter, deep and ancient wounds lose much of their old, old hurting. A crown is placed over our heads that for the rest of our lives we are trying to grow tall enough to wear. Despite all the crassness of life, despite all the harshness of life, life is saved by the singing of angels.[11]

A crown was placed on their heads! The shepherds no longer saw themselves as others viewed them. They weren't expendable or inconvenient, they were God's beloved children. Of all the people in the vicinity of Bethlehem, God chose *them* to witness the Messiah's birth. Life would never be the same, for they had heard the angels sing. "The shepherds returned, glorifying and praising God for all they had heard and seen, just as it had been told them."

CONTEMPLATION

The author of the Letter to the Hebrews counsels, "Do not neglect to show hospitality to strangers, for by doing that some have entertained angels without knowing it" (Hebrews 13:2). The word *angel* meant simply "messenger"—and the world is full of messages from God. Listen for the sounds of the angelic and the glory of angelic presence throughout the day. Look beneath the surface of life for messages and messengers, delivering Divine inspiration, guidance, and consolation. Pause throughout the day to look beyond appearances, to the light and love within. Look for the angelic in companion animals as well as fellow humans.

Give thanks for God's glory residing in all things, and for senses to experience the wonder of all being. Bring forth beauty and joy wherever you find it, so that you might be an angel to others, helping them realize their own crowns, the glory of God that is their identity and destiny.

God of angelic messengers,

astonished shepherds, amazed parents,

I long for radical amazement.

I long to see the Light that shines in all things.

I desire to experience the Holiness in all creation.

Open the doors of perception

that I might see Infinity in the here and now,

and love in every passing moment. Amen.

A DEMOCRACY
OF REVELATION

In the time of King Herod, after Jesus was born in
Bethlehem of Judea, magi from the east came to
Jerusalem, asking, "Where is the child who has been born
king of the Jews? For we observed his star in the east and
have come to pay him homage." When King Herod heard
this, he was frightened, and all Jerusalem with him, and
calling together all the chief priests and scribes of the
people, he inquired of them where the Messiah was to
be born. They told him, "In Bethlehem of Judea, for so it
has been written by the prophet: And you, Bethlehem, in
the land of Judah, are by no means least among the rulers
of Judah, for from you shall come a ruler who is to shepherd my people Israel.

Then Herod secretly called for the magi and learned
from them the exact time when the star had appeared. Then
he sent them to Bethlehem, saying, "Go and search diligently

for the child, and when you have found him, bring me word so that I may also go and pay him homage." When they had heard the king, they set out, and there, ahead of them, went the star that they had seen in the east, until it stopped over the place where the child was. When they saw that the star had stopped, they were overwhelmed with joy. On entering the house, they saw the child with Mary his mother, and they knelt down and paid him homage. Then, opening their treasure chests, they offered him gifts of gold, frankincense, and myrrh. And having been warned in a dream not to return to Herod, they left for their own country by another road. (Matthew 2:1–12)

There is no room for tribalism exalting a particular culture, ethnicity, race, or religion in the deep incarnation described in the Christmas stories. White Christian nationalists beware: God comes in the son of a Jewish carpenter and is visited by Mesopotamian, most likely Persian (ancestors of today's Iranians) spiritual guides! Magi from the East come to Jerusalem, expecting to receive guidance from the religious leaders about the location of the Messiah's birth. While the exact identities of the magis, or astrologers, is unclear, most scholarship points to their vocation as Zoroastrian or Zarathustrian spiritual leaders. Believing cosmic and Earth history involves the dynamic conflict between good and evil, darkness and light, the magi were astonished by the bright star in the East. They believed that the movements of the heavens reveal Divine order and intelligence and can also be portents of dramatic revelations of God. The bright star created a big stir, revealing what the magi believed to be the coming of the King of the Jews.

Despite their education and affluence, the magi were outsiders, ethnically and religiously. They belonged, according to the mainstream of first-century Judaism, to an inferior race and religion, and yet, to the chagrin of the Jerusalem religious hierarchy, they received a Divine revelation. They saw what the religious leaders missed: a star signaling that God was about to do a new thing to fulfill God's prophesy to the Jewish people and the world. The star gave notice that God's Light was coming to Earth and that a new world order would be emerging.

No doubt the magi were surprised at the apparent ignorance of the religious leaders. As keepers of the faith, they surely should be attentive to the coming of their Messiah! Instead, foreigners and outsiders received the revelation of God's incarnation. God is present in all things and revelation is both global and intimate, but we need to train our senses to intuit unique manifestations of Divine activity in our personal and planetary lives.

When they arrived at Jesus' home—not likely the stable of Bethlehem, since their arrival was probably a year or two later—the magi were overjoyed and paid homage to the Child. The magi recognize Jesus as God's Beloved Child and World-Changer. Then, while they returned home as his followers, there is no indication that they abandoned their own Zarathustrian faith.

It might surprise conservative Christians to know that the New Testament contains many passages that suggest Divine revelation is global and universal as well as personal. The Word and Wisdom of God range beyond Christianity to embrace all creation and people in every culture. God's incarnation is not limited to the Christian scriptures, sacraments, or civilization. John's Gospel proclaims that "the true light, which enlightens *everyone*, was coming into the world" (John 1:9, emphasis mine). When speaking with some Greeks, the apostle Paul affirms God's omnipresence and care that all persons find truth and salvation: "For 'In him we live and move and have our being'; as even some of your own poets have said, 'For we, too, are his offspring'" (Acts 17:28).

The magi were interspiritual adventurers, embracing the wisdom of the Christ Child while affirming the truths of their own tradition. In words also used to describe the young Jesus, they grew in wisdom and stature through their encounter with a star and a dream. They followed God's vision even if it meant going beyond their religious roots. Today, some of us follow the path of the magi in our integration of our Christian faith with spiritual practices from other spiritual traditions, such as meditation, yoga, mindfulness, and Reiki healing touch.

Stature is essential to religious maturity. Spirituality, at its best, enlarges our world and opens us to new possibilities. Revelation becomes greater and wider, and other religions and cultures become sources of inspiration and insight. Theologian Bernard Loomer, one of my graduate school professors, describes the process of growing in wisdom and stature:

> By size I mean the stature of a person's soul, the range and depth of his love, his capacity for relationships. I mean the volume of life you can take into your being and still maintain your integrity and individuality, the intensity and variety of outlook you can entertain in the unity of your being without feeling defensive or insecure. I mean the strength of your spirit to encourage others to become freer in the development of their diversity and uniqueness.[12]

Stature, or spiritual size, is at the heart of the journey of the magi. These interspiritual explorers trusted God—the One they called *Ahura Mazda*—and the insights of their personal faith enough to explore new spiritual horizons. No doubt, like the shepherds, they were forever changed. Perhaps, as their journeys continued, they discovered other stars to guide their spiritual adventure as they traveled always toward the Light that enlightens us all.

CONTEMPLATION

I grew up listening to Jiminy Cricket singing "When You Wish Upon a Star" in Disney's *Pinocchio*. We all need a star to guide us and a horizon to beckon us toward new adventures. God has planted stars on our horizon. We just need to look.

Take time to star gaze. Even in urban areas, you can glimpse a few stars shining in the heavens. Notice the stars that twinkle and catch your attention. Moving inward, invite God to place a star on your horizon. Ask God to show you a bright star to move you forward personally, spiritually, or politically. Notice stars, and when insights come, follow them.

The magi were interspiritual adventurers who invite us to broaden the horizons of our religious experiences through dialogue with the insights and practices of other wisdom traditions. My spiritual life has been broadened and deepened by my encounter with Buddhists, Hindus, Transcendentalists, and also, during my teen years, psychedelic pioneers. As a first-year college student in 1980, I learned Transcendental Meditation, which inspired me to study Christian mystics.

Jerry Jampolsky's and Susan Trout's vision of Attitudinal Healing, inspired by *A Course in Miracles,* a "New-Age" spiritual text, reintroduced me to the healing ministry of Jesus and the interplay of spirituality and medicine. In the mid-1980s, I became a practitioner of Reiki Healing Touch, and in the mid-1990s I became a Reiki teacher-master, integrating Jesus' healing with Japanese energy work. I am deeply Christian, committed to the way of Jesus, and my Christian faith has opened me to the insights of other faith traditions.

In this exercise, consider prayerfully the impact of other religious traditions on your spiritual growth. Where, if at all, have you gained from encounters with persons or practices from other faiths? Ask for Divine guidance about ways you can dialogue and learn from, as well as share, with persons of other wisdom traditions, trusting Jesus to guide your spiritual adventures.

God of light and darkness,
starry, starry nights, and bright sunny days,
place a star on my horizon.
Help me to grow, in breadth and depth,
and wisdom and stature,
giving glory to you while I offer light
for my neighbor's path.
In the name of the Child of Light. Amen.

POWERS AND PRINCIPALITIES

> When King Herod heard [the magis' message], he was frightened, and all Jerusalem with him, and calling together all the chief priests and scribes of the people, he inquired of them where the Messiah was to be born. . . . Then he sent [the magi] to Bethlehem, saying, "Go and search diligently for the child, and when you have found him, bring me word so that I may also go and pay him homage." . . . When Herod saw that he had been tricked by the magi, he was infuriated, and he sent and killed all the children in and around Bethlehem who were two years old or under, according to the time that he had learned from the magi. (Matthew 2:4, 8, 16)

King Herod hoped to preempt any threats to his power. The wily potentate sought to trick the magi into revealing the location of Jesus' residence, not for the sake of worship and adoration, but to murder the Child. God, however, is always wiser than the machinations of those who plan evil, and a dream warns the magi to return home without stopping at Jerusalem. The magi follow Divine guidance, and the Child is saved. Angry at their deception, Herod deploys his military to kill every baby and toddler in the vicinity of Bethlehem.

Herod's concern is with maintaining power and preserving his relationship with Rome. He will do anything to stay in power, even killing children. Herod's diabolical machinations remind us that institutions and their leaders can commit evil, and the evil of institutions must be confronted and denounced by prophetic voices to ensure liberty and justice, safety and equality for all.

The Incarnation of Jesus the Christ cannot be separated from the diabolical machinations of Herod and the Roman Empire. Although John in his Gospel celebrates the Light that illumines all people, he soberly recognizes that some turn from the Light to pursue the devices and desires of their own hearts, preferring the ways of darkness over the Light of God. In John's words: "He was in the world, and the world came into being through him, yet the world did not know him. He came to what was his own, and his own people did not accept him" (John 1:10–11).

While we must always remember the beauty of darkness as a place of growth and affirm God's presence in all the colors of the rainbow, including all the shades from white to black, many persons choose chaos and violence over the Light that the Bible describes. Not only individuals but institutions can be agents of death and destruction. The Hebraic prophets were particularly attentive to the impact of economic decisions made at a corporate level, and Jesus was crucified by the religious and political powers of his time, both Jewish and Roman. When presidents, kings, and caesars act, they don't act for themselves alone; they channel the spirit of their people and act on behalf of their nations. Empires can destroy, persecute, and oppress; they can also seek justice and equality, and redress the harm done by previous generations.

As I noted earlier, the personal is the political and the political and economic is always personal. Corporate profits skyrocket while everyday people struggle to make ends meet. Cost-cutting measures put thousands out of work and on the brink of poverty. Failure to consider the common good or look toward the well-being of future generations puts the planet in jeopardy. Hebrew Bible scholar and theologian Walter Wink asserts that in a Divinely ordered universe there is also room for human decision-making and agency: "The powers are good. The powers are fallen. The powers can be redeemed."[13]

The Gospel writers knew well the realities of political violence. They knew that Roman rule created a whole industry of graft and fraud, evident in the schemes of tax collectors and toll collectors. They also knew that the Temple was complicit in maintaining Roman law and order (another term for violent occupation and suppression of dissent), and that Temple leaders made profits from the fees charged for sacrifices. The Temple's exploitation of the poor for financial gain led Jesus to scatter the coins and overturn the tables of the money changers and Temple salespersons. Eventually, state and Temple collaborated in the crucifixion of Jesus.

There is always an element of coercion necessary to secure the peace and prosperity of a nation. National well-being requires the right balance of law and punishment, whether it involves sobriety on the road, paying taxes, obeying the rules of the road, or protecting the nation's borders. Nations and police use the threat of violence to prevent foreign intervention and crime in the streets. Still, the threat and use of violence must be governed by morality and mercy. Without moral and legal restraints on the use of power, there is disorder in streets, danger on the roads, violence against minorities, and threats against democracy. Nations are judged by their care for the "least of these" (Matthew 25:40).

Politicians, historians, and spiritual guides speak of healing the soul of America. The same aspiration is found among prophets in every land. Too often, the leaders of nations have led their countries to follow the evil, rather than the good, angels of their nature. What was intended to bring people together, whether a national constitution or a social media platform, has become a vehicle of hatred, incivility, and violence. Founded on the dream of all *men* created equal and endowed with basic rights, the United States destroyed First American culture and appropriated Native lands, perpetrated slavery on Africans and continued Jim (and modern-day James) Crow policies long after the abolition of slavery, stifled the voices and rights of women, and marginalized and persecuted the LGBTQ+ community. Politicians and corporate leaders have preferred short-term profits to the long-term well-being of communities and the planet. The powers that be have turned away from the paths of justice. They are in need of healing, so that they can once more be agents in God's quest for Shalom.

CONTEMPLATION

In this spiritual exercise, prayerfully consider your nation's current political and economic situation. You might begin with a time of prayer, then turn on the headline news on a trusted news outlet, listen to the pain and injustice being reported (the news beneath the news), and ask for guidance in responding. For example, recently, after another mass shooting at a U.S. school, I found myself feeling angry and hopeless about national change. My anger only grew as I observed the U.S. Senate putting the will of gun lobbies and an outdated view of the Second Amendment above the safety of school children, shoppers, concertgoers, and church attendees. I prayed about what I could do, given my talents and commitments. Living in a state where our representatives and laws support responsible gun ownership, I did not have to call my representatives or protest at their offices. I was inspired instead to write a short article in my monthly column on retired pastors' responses to gun violence for my denomination's pension board newsletter. I realize that this is a small beginning, but nevertheless, it's an expression of my talents to respond to the nation's needs.

In a time of reflection, consider where you may need to take seriously hymnist Harry Emerson Fosdick's prayer, "Save us from weak resignation to the evils we deplore." Let images of injustice and pain scroll before your eyes, as you reflect on your own feelings of despair and powerlessness. Invite God to reveal steps you may take to move from hopelessness and passivity to action and agency in your current community. Give thanks for the opportunity to have a role in shaping your community.

God of all peoples and places,
thank you for the good
that governments and institutions do
to preserve peace and provide healthy order.
Help me to look deeply at my institutions and government,
challenging them when they go astray.
Let me be an agent of prophetic healing and justice.
In the Name of the One who brings peace. Amen.

LISTEN TO YOUR CHILDREN CRYING

Then what had been spoken through the prophet Jeremiah was fulfilled:

> A voice was heard in Ramah,
> wailing and loud lamentation,
> Rachel weeping for her children;
> she refused to be consoled,
> because they are no more. (Luke 2:17–18)

Uvalde, Parkland, Columbine, Sandy Hook: God, listen to your children crying. Somalia, Ethiopia, Syria, Afghanistan, Ukraine: God, listen, to your children praying.

The powers and principalities often have little true concern for the well-being of the most vulnerable. They embrace the rights of fetuses for political gain, even as they reveal their actual indifference by eliminating programs for babies and children. Grief and anguish abound. Rachel shares her tears with the parents of Ramah, Uvalde, Newtown, and every town that must face the terrible reality that their children's deaths were caused by national policies and corporate decision-making.

The parents of Ramah were inconsolable. Their children didn't have to die. Herod's troops didn't have to raze the next generation just to keep an old man in power. The parents of Sandy Hook and Uvalde are in despair. Their children didn't have to die. A teenager didn't have to fire shots from an automatic rifle just to satisfy a convoluted understanding of freedom and the gun lust of the nation. God, listen to your children crying. God, listen to your children praying for a new world order, where apathy is transformed to empathy, where power and privilege are trumped by compassion and care.

Herod was afraid and he took it out on the "least of these," the ones who could not protect themselves, vulnerable infants and children, the powerless mothers, and impoverished communities. These infants died instead of the infant Jesus.

The memory of the massacre of the children may have haunted Jesus all his life. He knew that he survived while others perished. Perhaps, as a child and teenager, he wondered about the mystery of suffering: *Why did I survive when others didn't?* Jesus' "survivor's guilt" may have shaped his understanding of the relationship between God and suffering. He knew that sin could be a factor in illness, but he did not claim a one-to-one correspondence between morality and fortune. He did not judge the sick or wayward but healed them and challenged them to personal transformation.

When confronted by a sight-impaired man, Jesus' followers asked, "Rabbi, who sinned, this man or his parents, that he was born blind?" and Jesus answered, "Neither this man nor his parents sinned; he was born blind so that God's works might be revealed in him." Still, Jesus doesn't seem to be satisfied by his own answer that, at first glance, focuses on the positive consequences that will come out of his healing of the man's blindness. Instead, he responds, "We must work the works of him who sent me while it is day; night is coming, when no one can work. As long as I am in the world, I am the light of the world." Then, Jesus spits on the ground, makes some mud, a first-century medicinal remedy, and cures the man (John 9:1–7). Jesus shows us that the proper spiritual response to the problem of evil is constructive action to relieve suffering rather than abstract theological speculation which does nothing to ease the pain of those who suffer.

Perhaps the tears of Rachel reminded Jesus, in the spirit of Job, to tell us that suffering can be arbitrary, a matter of luck, being at the wrong place at the wrong time; God does not dispense pain to one and not another. Jesus recognized that the universe and human life reflect a combination of chance and intention, chaos and wisdom, malfeasance and kindness. Love manifest in healing action is the answer to the suffering we observe.

> But I say to you: Love your enemies and pray for those who persecute you, so that you may be children of your Father in heaven, for he makes his sun rise on the evil and on the good and sends rain on the righteous and on the unrighteous. (Matthew 5:44–45)

Jesus responded to those persons who were smug in their righteousness, believing that their morality or special relationship with God would exempt them from the slings and arrows of misfortune:

> At that very time there were some present who told Jesus about the Galileans whose blood Pilate had mingled with their sacrifices. He asked them, "Do you think that because these Galileans suffered in this way they were worse sinners than all other Galileans? No, I tell you, but unless you repent you will all perish as they did. Or those eighteen who were killed when the

tower of Siloam fell on them—do you think that they were worse offenders than all the other people living in Jerusalem? No, I tell you, but unless you repent you will all perish just as they did." (Luke 13:1–5)

The reality of death and the arbitrariness of suffering are not God-caused but a challenge to repentance, to transform our lives and turn to God's way. God's goal is that all people have an abundant life (John 10:10). When we choose death and destruction over life and creativity for ourselves and others, then Rachel weeps, parents mourn, and children perish. More than that, God weeps. God feels our pain. God is the fellow-sufferer who understands and the loving companion who celebrates. God is present in our suffering, feeling it from the inside out. God is also present in challenging us to respond to suffering, to move from self-interest to world loyalty.

God mourns what could have been if only we listened to the children crying and God weeping with them. The stories of children massacred by the machinations of politicians and corporate executives and the cries of mourning parents should make us mourn as well. Like Jesus, we are challenged to use our pain and anger to confront the perpetrators of violence (who often wear suits, ties, and white collars, or judges' robes) to mend their ways and join with God in healing the nation and the planet.

CONTEMPLATION

Today's spiritual practice builds on Meditation Ten. This time, though, take time to listen prayerfully to the children crying. As you read your newsfeed or attend to the news on radio, television, or livestream, notice the impact of public policies on children. Where are national and local policies helping children live abundant lives? Where are national and local policies harming children? Where are parents rejoicing and where are parents mourning? Then, from your listening, let your emotions rise as a prayer for guidance and courage. While political solutions may be complicated and opaque, nevertheless we cannot stand aside. Our empathy must be translated into prayerful responsiveness in our citizenship. This may eventuate in confronting local school boards and town councils—or challenging political leaders through petitions, protests, and phone calls. We may decide to be the hands, feet, and heart of God through volunteering in programs that support children: tutoring at a school, coaching a team, advocating change through the Children's Defense Fund or the Poor People's March. As the Talmud states, "Do not be daunted by the enormity of the world's grief. Do justly now, love mercy now, walk humbly now. You are not obligated to complete the work, but neither are you free to abandon it."

God of empathy and imagination,
companionship and challenge,
move us from apathy to empathy
and from empathy to activism.
Let your love spark within us love for all your children.
Let us not turn away from the pain of the world,
but instead claim our role as your fellow-healers
in the restoration of our nation and the planet.
In Christ's name. Amen.

HOME BY ANOTHER WAY

And having been warned in a dream not to return to Herod, they [the magi] left for their own country by another road. . . . Now after they had left, an angel of the Lord appeared to Joseph in a dream and said, "Get up, take the child and his mother, and flee to Egypt, and remain there until I tell you, for Herod is about to search for the child, to destroy him." Then Joseph got up, took the child and his mother by night, and went to Egypt and remained there until the death of Herod. This was to fulfill what had been spoken by the Lord through the prophet, "Out of Egypt I have called my son."

When Herod died, an angel of the Lord suddenly appeared in a dream to Joseph in Egypt and said, "Get up, take the child and his mother, and go to the land of Israel, for those who were seeking the child's life are dead." Then Joseph got up, took the child and his mother, and went to the land of Israel. But when he heard that Archelaus was ruling Judea in place of his father Herod, he was afraid to go there. And after being warned in a dream, he went away to the district of Galilee. There he made his home in a town called Nazareth, so that what had been spoken through the prophets might be fulfilled, "He will be called a Nazarene." (Matthew 2:12–15, 19–23)

One of the most evocative passages in scripture describes the response of the magi to their collective dream: "And having been warned in a dream not to return to Herod, [the magi] left for their own country by another road." The magi went home by another way. They had planned to return to Herod with news of their visit, but when God spoke to them through a dream, they changed their plans, reoriented their spiritual and geographical GPS, and bypassed the crafty and violent Herod, thus preventing the violent ruler from killing the infant Jesus.

The adventure of the magi describes the unpredictability of the human journey. You plan a future, but an unexpected circumstance requires you to change your plans, look for a new job, find a new home, reevaluate your priorities, or respond to tragedy. The magi, no doubt, wrestled with what they should do and with the inconvenience of choosing a new route. But, because they believed that God speaks in dreams as well as stars, they altered their course, arriving home by the road less traveled, the improvised pathway.

Joseph also must change course. He has to alter his life plan, not only to marry Mary but to flee the country. He assumed he would return to Nazareth, go back to work, and raise a family. But a dream can change everything: he takes his family to Egypt to settle as a stranger and immigrant in a strange land.

A few years later, Joseph receives another guiding dream, telling him that it's time to return home. Intending to return to Judea, Joseph discerns intuitively that Judea is unsafe for his young son. At the right time, Joseph has another dream, telling him that it will be safe to settle in Nazareth, and that his young child will flourish and grow into manhood, learning carpentry at his father's side.

Joseph's path home was drawn out and circuitous. Listening to his dreams and reorienting his pathway, however, saved the infant Jesus. Within the interruptions and inconveniences of our lives as well, God is at work. While God is not the source of sickness, death, job loss, and political threat, "in all things God works for good" (Romans 8:28). When we follow God's vision, we will discover a way when we previously saw no way. God makes a way in the wilderness, when we let go of our plans and open to God's larger vision for us and our future.

Twice I have been professionally devastated by unexpected job losses. I worried that I might follow in my father's footsteps and never recover professionally from having my positions eliminated, despite my previously successful work. I discovered that, despite my uncertainty and fear, when I imagined new futures and took new routes, I found resiliency and creativity that opened unexpected and positive paths toward the future. When I opened to God's wisdom, new energies and insights emerged. I discovered new talents, and in each time of transition, I experienced an influx of imagination and creativity. It wasn't easy to make significant professional changes. Failure was always a possibility. But I trusted that in companionship with God, listening to God's guidance, a path to the future would open—and it did! God truly made a way when I initially saw no way forward. Incarnation happens in the messiness and conflict of life.

Jesus' birth is accompanied by tragedy. His family must run for their lives, even as other children are slaughtered. God did not predestine Herod's antipathy and violence, nor did God choose the massacre of the infants. But within the conflicts of history, God is with us. Within our uncertainty, a light shines, joining the cradle and cosmos, the finite and infinite. Following that light, we will find our way home.

Diogenes, a wise fourth-century Greek philosopher, wrote, "It will be solved in the walking." We will also find God's way in the walking. We may not always know where the journey will take us, but when we claim Jesus as our companion, we will find, one step at a time, the way, the truth, and the life in our place and time.

CONTEMPLATION

In this spiritual exercise, take a walk, either imaginatively or physically, depending on your health condition and the weather. Begin your walk with a prayer for Divine guidance as you lift up a problem or decision that lies before you. Breathe deeply, opening yourself to insight and inspiration. Let thoughts and images flow, and take your insights prayerfully to God. Take note of the environment and the beauty that surrounds you, giving thanks for God's creation and your own unique life.

Listen throughout the days ahead for insights and inspirations, trusting that God will make a way for your future adventures.

God of the journey,

make me open to new ways;

help me to abandon the paths that prove to be dead ends,

knowing that your creative power

is at work in each circumstance,

weaving all things together for good

in ways I cannot imagine.

Teach me to seek your messages to me.

Keep me open to dreams and strangers.

Give me the strength and courage I need

to work with you to build

your Realm of Shalom here on Earth.

In the name of the Life-Giver. Amen

FROM CRADLE TO COSMOS AND BACK

Let the same mind be in you that was in Christ Jesus, who, though he existed in the form of God, did not regard equality with God as something to be grasped, but emptied himself, taking the form of a slave, assuming human likeness. And being found in appearance as a human, he humbled himself and became obedient to the point of death—even death on a cross. (Philippians 2:5–11)

From cosmos to cradle, the entire universe conspires to create each moment of experience. God is incarnate in the world of the flesh, calling us to wholeness, in every encounter and action. From cradle to cosmos, the cry of a vulnerable baby touches the heart of God. Each newborn bears the visage of Divinity. One unique first-century Jewish child reveals the moral and spiritual heart of the universe and shows us what we can be if we incarnate his values in our daily lives and personal and political decision-making. The Infinite gives birth to the finite, and the finite shapes Infinity. The cradle embodies the moral and spiritual arcs of the cosmos and reveals the heart of God. The Word and Wisdom of God gives birth to all creation. We, in return, are the midwives of God, bringing God's realm to earth as it is in heaven.

On Easter, we sing, "Christ the Lord is Risen Today." That means today. Now is the day of resurrection and salvation. At Christmas, we sing, "Be born in us today. . . . O Come to us, abide with us, our Lord Emmanuel." In response, we can daily proclaim, "This is the day that God has made," the day of healing, wholeness, salvation, and grace. The day in which we can feed the hungry and turn weapons of war into agricultural implements.

The Incarnation is the message of Christmas: God is with us, the Word becomes flesh in first-century history and politics, as well as in the history and politics of our time. We are each in the "thin place" where the Infinite and finite meet in intimate creativity. We too are Mary and Joseph, the shepherd, the magi, and the angelic visitors. To our dismay, we are also Herod. We turn from the light. We fail to see the star and choose self-interest over the survival of the vulnerable. And yet, still, Christ is born in us, giving us strength for today and bright hope for the future in God's never-ending adventure of incarnation. The darkness and chaos cannot defeat God's light, and despite our waywardness, there is always the promise of light to guide our footsteps home.

Cosmos and cradle are one movement. God is with us, saying, "Don't be afraid. Be a light in the world. Bring beauty and healing to the good Earth I created."

> When the song of the angels is stilled,
> When the star in the sky is gone,
> When the kings and princes are home,
> When the shepherds are back with their flock,
> The work of Christmas begins:
> To find the lost,
> To heal the broken,
> To feed the hungry,
> To release the prisoner, . . .
> To bring peace among brothers.[14]

Let us all say, "Amen."

NOTES

1. "Shalom" is a biblical concept that goes far beyond its common translation as "peace." Shalom is God's Realm on earth, a realm of completeness, wholeness, health, peace, welfare, safety, soundness, tranquility, prosperity, perfectness, fullness, rest, well-being, and harmony—for all people.

2. Dag Hammarskjold. *Markings* (New York: Knopf, 1964), p. 169.

3. Howard Thurman. *The Growing Edge* (Richmond, IN: Friends United Press, 1956), p. 180.

4. See interview in "Rabbi Heschel on the Via Positiva," *Daily Meditations with Matthew Fox* (August 5, 2019), https://dailymeditationswithmatthewfox.org/2019/08/05/rabbi-heschel-on-the-via-positiva-part-2/.

5. I have appreciated Crossan's and Borg's discussion of the two genealogies (Matthew 1:1–17 and Luke 3:23–38) in *First Christmas: What the Gospels Really Teach About Jesus' Birth* (New York: HarperOne, 2007), pp. 81–98.

6. Hammarskjold, p. 89.

7. See John Sanford's *Dreams: God's Forgotten Language* (San Francisco, CA: HarperOne, 1989).

8. John Dominic Crossan. *Jesus: A Revolutionary Biography* (San Francisco, CA: HarperOne, 2009).

9. Ibid.

10. "Shepherd Status," by Randy Alcorn, in *Come, Thou Long-Expected Jesus,* Nancy Guthrie, ed. (Wheaton, IL: Crossway Books, 2008), pp. 85–89.

11. Howard Thurman. *The Mood of Christmas and Other Celebrations* (Richmond, IN: Friends United Press, 1985), p. 10.

12. Harry James Cargas and Bernard Lee. *Religious Experience and Process Theology* (Mahweh, NJ: Paulist Press. 1976), p 70.

13. Walter Wink. *Engaging the Powers* (Philadelphia, PA: Fortress Press, 1992), p. 65.

14. Thurman. *The Mood of Christmas and Other Celebrations,* p. 23.

Thin Places Everywhere

The 12 Days of Christmas with Celtic Christianity

Bruce Epperly invites you to share a Christmas adventure with him, voyaging through the 12 days of Christmas (plus Christmas Eve and Epiphany) with Brendan, Columba, Brigid, Patrick, and other Celtic saints. With these Celtic adventurers as your companions, you will discover "thin places"—moments of time when the Incarnation of Christ shines through ordinary people, places, and events. After the busyness of Advent, the days that follow Christmas can be a quieter time, when you can venture out on an inner vision quest for new ways of seeing and being.

Loving God, give me vision. Help me hear the singing of angels and the crying of children. Let my prayers take shape in loving words and healing hands. Walk with me, and help me walk with the lost and lonely, the forgotten and marginalized. Let my life be an incarnation of that little Child who is our Savior.

The Work of Christmas

The 12 Days of Christmas with Howard Thurman

This book is a celebration of the twelve days of Christmas, offering us a chance to dwell on the meaning of the season in dialog with the wisdom of one of America's greatest mystics and activists, Howard Thurman.

Thurman knew that Christmas always begins in darkness—the darkness of the womb, the darkness of human violence and oppression, the darkness of hopelessness. In Christmas, Thurman reminds us, a light shines even in the darkness, and

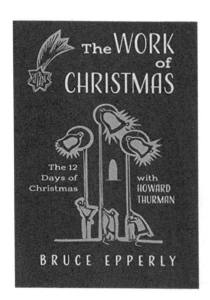

this light will never be defeated. God's light streams into the most unexpected places—a stable, among foreign magi from another religious tradition, and in the varieties of human culture and ethnicity. Just a little light can transform the darkness and help us anxious pilgrims find our way.

I Wonder as I Wander

The 12 Days of Christmas with Madeleine L'Engle

How can we recover the radical meaning of the Christmas season? Using the thoughts and words of Madeleine L'Engle, this books offers you a guide through the hectic Christmas season. With quiet times of prayer, Scripture, and meditation, you can begin to wonder-to imagine big possibilities and ask important questions-as you wander outside your typical comfort zones. In the twelve days of Christmas, bookended by Christmas Eve and the Feast of Epiphany, you will experience anew the awe and wonder of the Incarnation.

As you both wonder and wander, the questions and images in this book will open your heart to the radical message of Christmas. Like the Magi, you too can follow a star, seeking wisdom in everyday life, while contemplating the cosmic forces within which we live and move and have our being.

Become Fire!
Guideposts for Interspiritual Pilgrims

In the spirit of God's call to creative transformation, Bruce Epperly invites you to join him on a holy adventure in spiritual growth, inspired by the evolving wisdom of Christianity and the world's great spiritual traditions, innovative global spiritual practices, and emerging visions of reality. Epperly explores the many resources of Christian spirituality in dialogue with the spiritual practices of the world's great wisdom traditions, describing the gifts other spiritual paths contribute to the pathway of Jesus; at the same time,

he uses the lens of the spiritual practices Jesus has inspired throughout Christian history to examine these spiritual paths. By embracing the diverse insights of spiritual wisdom givers, physicists, cosmologists, healing practitioners, and Earth keepers, we can meet the Earth's current challenges with love, joy, and a united strength.

Prepare the Way

Celtic Prayers for the Season of Light

Ray Simpson has given his life, both professionally and personally, to Celtic Christianity, and now he helps us to celebrate a Celtic outlook on the season of Christmas. With their eloquent yet simple words, his prayers welcome the Holy One who comes to us in small, ordinary ways, who is present in the helpless and the vulnerable. As we join Ray in prayer, we stand on the threshold to paradox and mystery—and we "prepare the way" for God to enter our world anew.

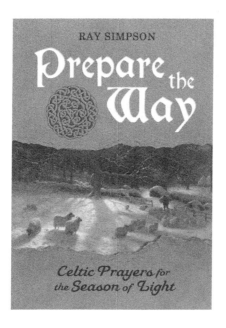

AnamcharaBooks.com

Made in United States
Orlando, FL
15 February 2024